MW01405882

THIS BOOK IS FOR

BORN

LOTS OF LOVE
FOREVER & ALWAYS

Made in the USA
Columbia, SC
29 November 2023

27426660R00083